One Rehearsal Wonders Vol. 5

ALMOST INSTANT ANTHEMS FOR ANY OCCASION

ISBN 9-781-5400-6073-0

EXCLUSIVELY DISTRIBUTED BY

Visit Hal Leonard Online at
www.halleonard.com

Visit Shawnee Press Online at
www.shawneepress.com

Contact us:
Hal Leonard
7777 West Bluemound Road
Milwaukee, WI 53213
Email: info@halleonard.com

In Europe, contact:
Hal Leonard Europe Limited
42 Wigmore Street
Marylebone, London, W1U 2RN
Email: info@halleonardeurope.com

In Australia, contact:
Hal Leonard Australia Pty. Ltd.
4 Lentara Court
Cheltenham, Victoria, 3192 Australia
Email: info@halleonard.com.au

THIS IS THE DAY!

for S.A.T.B. voices, accompanied

Words based on
Psalm 118:24

Music by
KEITH CHRISTOPHER (ASCAP)

4

6

10

GOD IS!

for S.A.(T.)B. voices and opt. flute (or C-inst.), accompanied*

Words by
BERT STRATTON (ASCAP)

Music by
MICHAEL BARRETT (BMI)

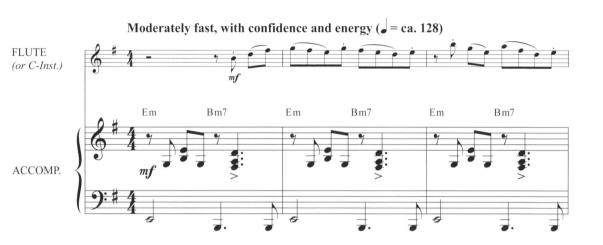

*Part for Flute (or C-instrument) available as a free download.
Visit halleonard.com, search for item 00299582 and click on the Closer Look icon to access the PDF.

12

God is Art-ist of the day and night,_

Rul-er o-ver ev-'ry-thing._

and He is the Au-thor of the Book of Life.__ He's the

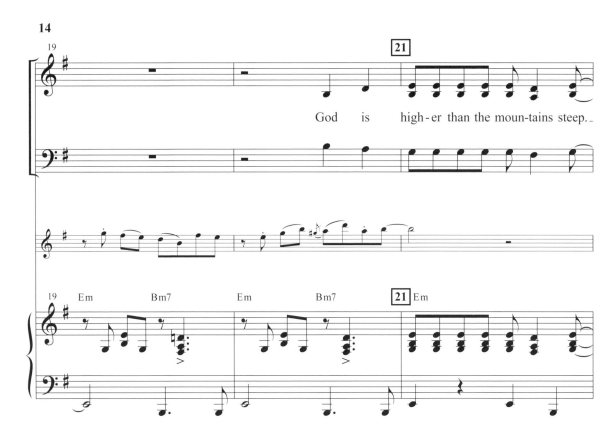

bright - er than the morn - ing sun._____ Just be - hold the

won - ders that His hands have done._____ He's a

16

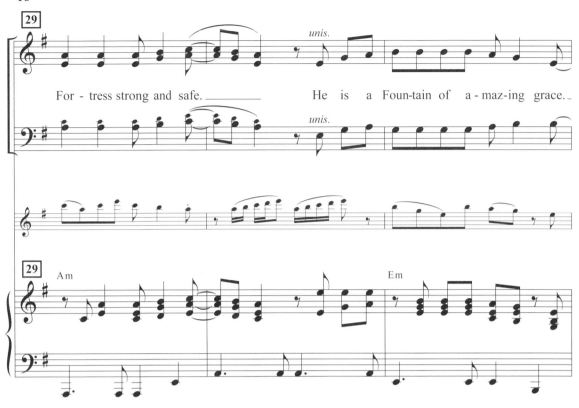

My God is might-y to be praised.

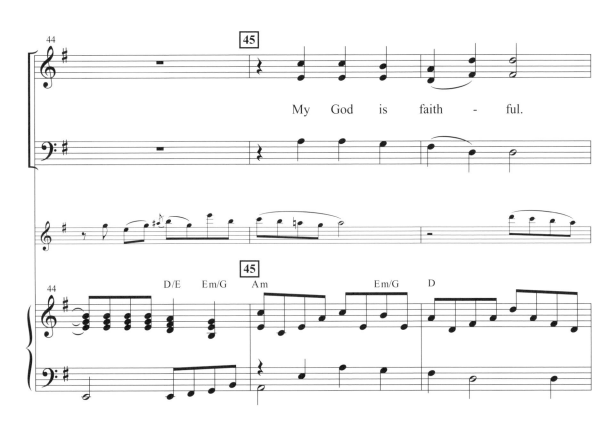

My God is faith - ful.

My God is ev - er sure. My God is

great in all His ways!

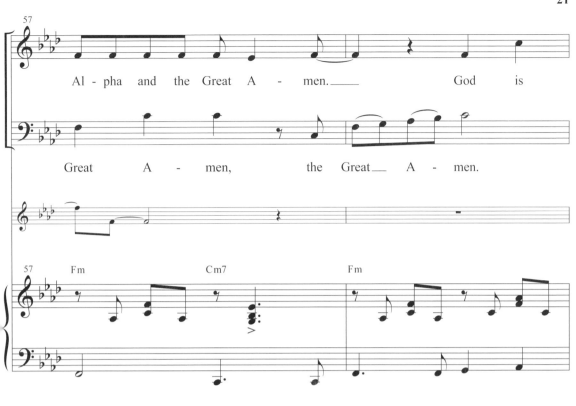

morn - ing stars to dance and sing._____ God is

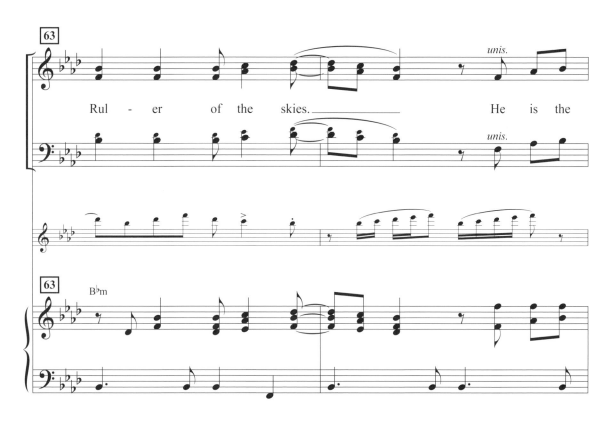

Rul - er of the skies._____ He is the

First and Last, the One most high!___ O

broth-er, let me tell you this:___ "My God is!" God is

Rul - er of the skies._____ He is the First and Last, the One most high!__

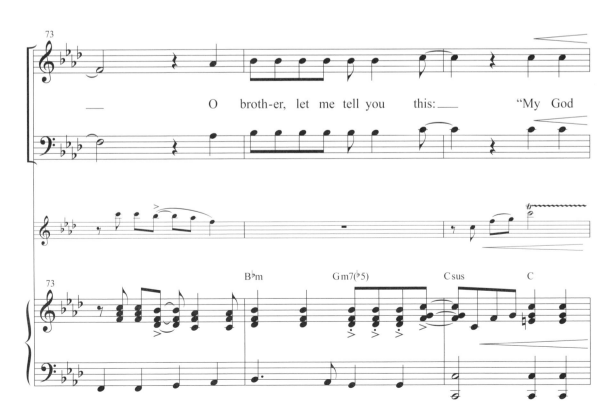

O broth-er, let me tell you this:___ "My God

ALL GOOD GIFTS

for S.A.B. voices, accompanied

Original Words by
MATTHIAS CLAUDIUS (1740-1815)
Tr. JANE M. CAMPBELL (1817-1878)

Music by
MICHAEL BARRETT (BMI)

28

hum - ble, thank - ful hearts.

All good gifts come from God a - bove,

All good gifts, all good

from God a - bove.

gifts come from God, our Fa - ther.

Then thank the Lord, __ O thank the Lord,

O thank the Lord for all __ His love.

O thank the Lord for all His love. __

Much slower

SING OUT, CHILDREN OF GOD

for S.A.T.B. voices, accompanied

Words by
MARY FOIL

Music by
MICHAEL BARRETT (BMI)

Copyright © 1997 by Malcolm Music, a div. of Shawnee Press, Inc.
International Copyright Secured All Rights Reserved

40

Come, chil - dren, lift your voice to heav - en.

For - ev - er bless the Lord and

serve Him all your days.

Al - le - lu -

AT THE TABLE OF THE LORD

for S.A.B. voices, accompanied

Words by
JOSEPH M. MARTIN (BMI)

Music by
JOSEPH M. MARTIN
and DAVID ANGERMAN (ASCAP)

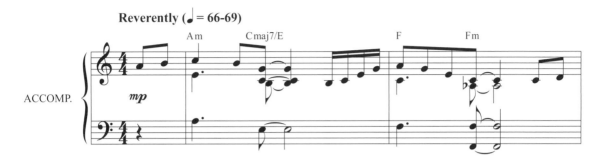

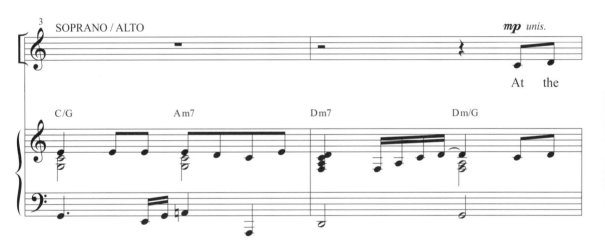

47

50

WONDERFUL LIGHT!

for 2-part mixed voices, accompanied

Arranged by
STEWART HARRIS (BMI)

Words and Music by
KAREN CRANE (ASCAP)

Christ brought me out of my dark - ness in - to won - der - ful light;

out of my weak - ness in - to all of His might; out of my sor - row and

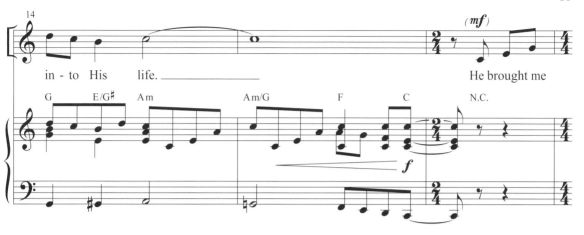

in - to His life. _____ He brought me

out of my dark - ness in - to won - der - ful light!

PART I

PART II

*A - maz - ing grace,_ how

55

O FOR A HEART

for S.A.B. voices, accompanied

Words by
CHARLES WESLEY (1707-1788)
Additional Words by
C.E. WALZ

Tune: **KELVINGROVE**
Traditional Scottish Melody
Arranged by
C.E. WALZ

60

a heart re-signed and meek, my__ great Re-deem-er's me: throne, where__ on - ly Christ is heard to speak, where Je - sus reigns a - lone. O - pen my heart, dear Lord.

nei - ther life nor death can part from Christ who dwells with - in: a

heart re - newed in thought, and___ full of love a -

lone; per - fect, right, pure and good, a cop - y of God's

64

COME TO ME, YOU WEARY

for S.A.T.B. voices, accompanied

Words by
PATRICIA MOCK (ASCAP)
Adaptation of "Come Unto Me, You Weary"
by WILLIAM CHATTERTON DIX (1837-1898)

Music by
PATRICIA MOCK
and JAMES MICHAEL STEVENS (ASCAP)
Arranged by
JAMES MICHAEL STEVENS

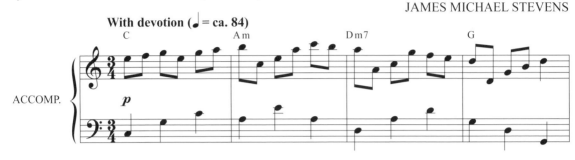

"Come to Me, you wea - ry, and I will give you rest."

Hear the words of Je - sus, who speaks to hearts, op - pressed, of

Come to Me, you faint - ing, and I will give you life." See the heart of Je - sus, who calms the storms and strife. He calls to us, our

LET US GIVE THANKS TO THE LORD

for S.A.B. voices, accompanied

Words by
ROGER THORNHILL (BMI)

Music by
BRAD NIX (ASCAP)
Incorporating
"For the Beauty of the Earth"

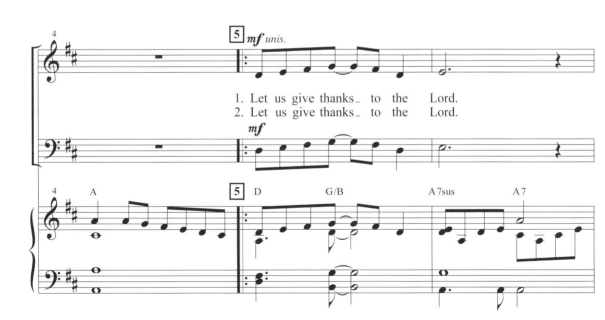

* Tune: DIX, Conrad Kocher, 1786-1872
Words: Folliott S. Pierpoint, 1835-1917

this, our hymn of grate - ful praise.

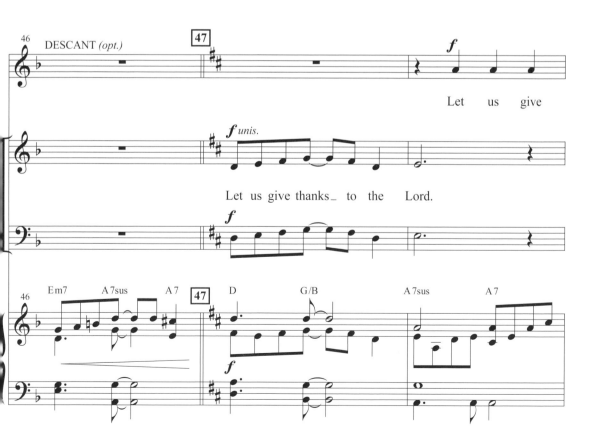

DESCANT (opt.)

Let us give

Let us give thanks to the Lord.

thanks. Give thanks with ju - bi - lant voice_ and

Let us give thanks_ to the Lord. With ju - bi - lant voice_ and

D G A 7sus A 7 G A/G

joy - ful noise,_ let us give thanks_ to the Lord.

unis.

joy - ful noise,_ let us give thanks_ to the Lord.

D/F♯ G/B Em7 G/A A 7 D

GRACE AND PEACE TO YOU

for S.A.T.B. voices, with opt. flute or violin, accompanied*

Words and Music by
DARCY STANLEY (ASCAP)

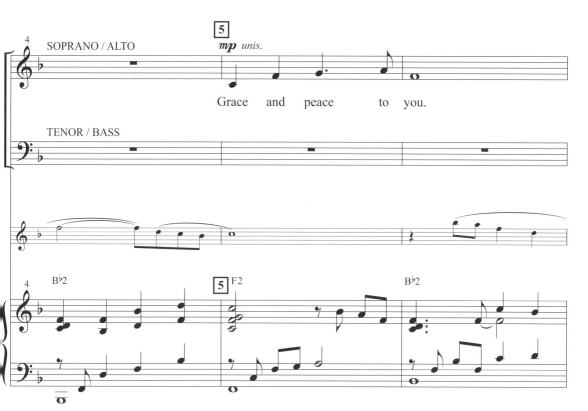

*Part for Flute or Violin available as a free download.
 Visit halleonard.com, search for item 00299582 and click on the Closer Look icon to access the PDF.

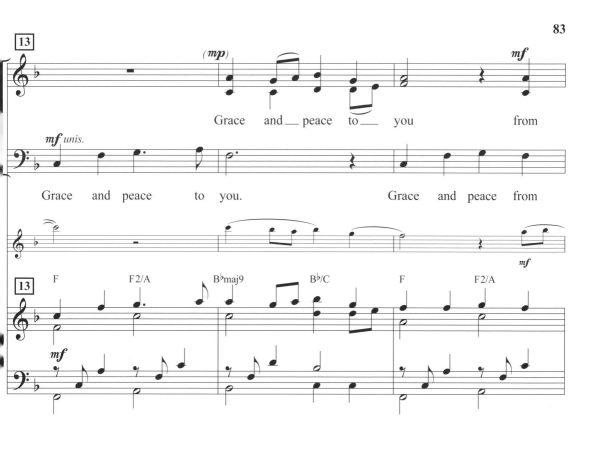

grace and peace to you.

Glo - ry to our

heav'n a - bove. Grace and peace to

Grace and peace to you.

you from God, our ___ Fa - ther. May His love shine

Grace and peace from God, our Fa - ther.

though His gift of grace and peace to

Am   Dm   Gm11   Gm11/B♭   B♭2/C

you.

F   F/E   Dm7   Dm7/C   B♭2

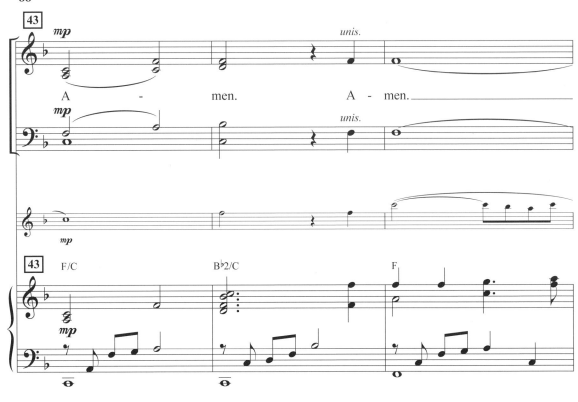

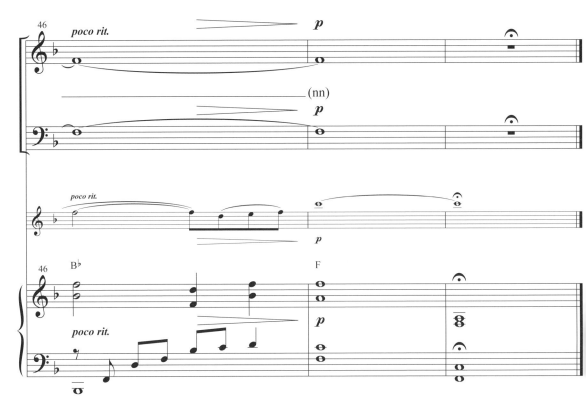